We wonder how animals live in the cold.
We wait for the first snowfall.
We wonder how snowflakes form.
We wait for some of our favorite holidays.

WE WAIT . . .

Winter begins on the winter solstice. In the Northern Hemisphere, that's a day near December 22. It's the shortest day of the year.

. . . FOR DAYS TO GET LONGER.

Winter ends on the vernal equinox. In the Northern Hemisphere, that's a day near March 20, when day and night are both 12 hours long.

WE WAIT . . .

When you want to go outside in winter, you can't just run out the door. Wearing many layers of clothing can help keep you warm, but putting everything on takes time.

. . . TO GO OUTSIDE.

Clothing layers create air spaces between your skin and the cold. These spaces insulate, which means they trap the heat from your body. You feel warmer because your body's heat stays in the spaces between layers.

OUTSIDE,
TREES WAIT FOR
WARMER
WEATHER.

In winter, a tree with no leaves isn't dead. It dropped its leaves in the fall because they would be too delicate to survive when it gets cold. Big, flat leaves would also hold too much snow and ice. The weight of all that snow could make branches break. Trees with bare branches can stay strong and save water during all kinds of winter weather.

Trees that drop their leaves in autumn are called deciduous trees.

OTHER TREES HAVE
A WONDERFUL WAY TO
STAY GREEN
ALL WINTER.

Evergreens have needles or
leaves that are covered with a heavy
wax that protects them. This wax keeps the
moisture in an evergreen from freezing.

Evergreen needles don't live forever. These trees are "ever green" because they are green all year round. Evergreen needles live for two to ten years before they drop to make way for fresh, new needles. Some evergreens lose most of their needles in autumn. Others shed old needles throughout the year.

HOW DOES WINTER FEEL?

cold

frosty

toasty

hard

icy

sharp

soft

cozy

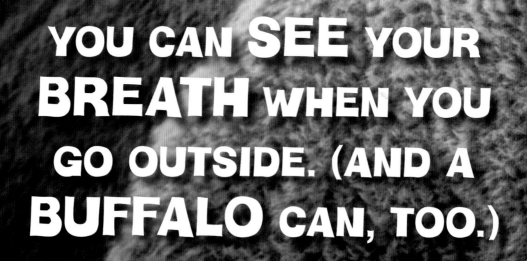

YOU CAN **SEE** YOUR **BREATH** WHEN YOU GO OUTSIDE. (AND A **BUFFALO** CAN, TOO.)

Your breath isn't empty air. It always contains some moisture, called water vapor. Warm air can hold more moisture than cold air. So when you exhale in warm weather, the water vapor in your breath mixes with the air and you don't see anything.

But when you exhale in cold weather, water vapor from your breath hits the cold air and condenses into tiny droplets of water and ice. Your breath—or a buffalo's—forms a cloud like a light fog.

bat

SOME ANIMALS WAIT FOR WARM WEATHER BY SLOWING DOWN.

Some small mammals—including chipmunks, woodchucks, hedgehogs, and several kinds of bats—hibernate in winter. These animals curl up tightly while hibernating. Their heartbeat decreases and their body temperature drops to be almost equal to the cold outside. They don't eat all winter long. Instead, they live off fat stored in their bodies. Every week or two, hibernators wake up and move around—but not for very long.

dormouse

hedgehog

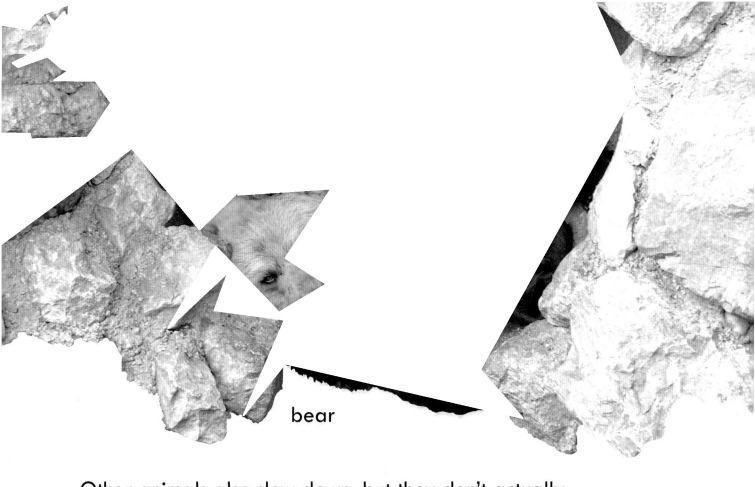

bear

Other animals also slow down, but they don't actually hibernate. These include bears, raccoons, skunks, and birds that don't fly to warmer places for the winter. These animals go into a very slow state called torpor. A torpor can last just a few hours, several days, or even weeks. Animals in torpor also drop their body temperature, but not as much as true hibernators. These animals might wake up when they are hungry or in danger.

raccoon

skunk

OTHER ANIMALS
KEEP MOVING
ALL WINTER LONG
TO FIND FOOD.

songbird

Animals like
beavers and some kinds
of squirrels and mice gather
extra food in the fall, but they still
hunt during the winter, too.

squirrel

beaver

moose

Rabbits, deer, moose, and many birds eat what they can find in winter, such as moss, leaves, twigs, bark, and seeds.

deer

Other animals, like the red fox, change their diet when winter comes. Most of the year, foxes eat fruits and insects. But in the winter when these foods are not available, they eat mice and other small rodents.

fox

ANIMALS HAVE SOME WONDERFUL WAYS TO HANDLE COLD WEATHER.

Animals adapt to the places where they live. Animals that live in cold areas are usually larger and heavier than similar animals living in warmer places. Polar bears are bigger than tropical bears. Deer in Michigan are larger than similar deer in Florida or Texas. The extra size and weight makes it easier for them to stay warm.

Body parts like legs
and ears can also adapt.
Long, thin body parts lose heat
quickly, so legs and ears are smaller
in animals that live in cold areas.
Snowshoe hares have smaller ears than
cottontail rabbits. Polar bears
have shorter, thicker legs and
snouts and smaller ears
than tropical bears.

WHAT DOES WINTER SOUND LIKE?

CRUNCH

CRACK

SCRAPE

BRRRRRRRR

IT'S SNOWING—
ONE OF WINTER'S
WONDERS!

Snow begins when
clouds get cold. Clouds are made
of water vapor. When the temperature
is 32°F (0°C) or lower, water vapor in
a cloud freezes and forms snowflakes.

A snowflake starts as a tiny ice crystal. Because
the crystal is heavier than air, it falls to the ground.
As an ice crystal falls, usually at a speed of
about three or four miles per hour, it connects
with other crystals, and the snowflake gets
bigger. By the time a snowflake
lands, it usually contains about
200 ice crystals.

Up close, a snowflake
looks clear, or sometimes blue.
So why does snow look white on the
ground? The same reason that a pile of
broken glass looks white. Light enters snow
and bounces around in all of those ice crystals.
The light we see reflected from snow includes
an equal mix of all colors. When you
mix all colors of light equally,
you get white light.

IS IT **TRUE** THAT NO TWO SNOWFLAKES ARE **ALIKE?**

A tiny, single ice crystal has six sides. As it connects with other crystals on the way down, the new crystals connect to these sides and form six arms, called dendrites. That's why most snowflakes have six sides. But that doesn't mean they're all alike.

A snowflake is a clump of many ice crystals. Every ice crystal is made of tiny parts called water molecules. These parts are much too small to see without a special microscope. One snowflake contains billions and billions of water molecules. Those tiny parts can be arranged in so many different ways that it's highly unlikely two snowflakes are exactly the same. In fact, it's unlikely two snowflakes have ever been exactly alike since snow first started falling on Earth.

WHAT SHAPE IS WINTER?

Six-sided snowflakes aren't the only shape you see in winter. What might you see that's round?

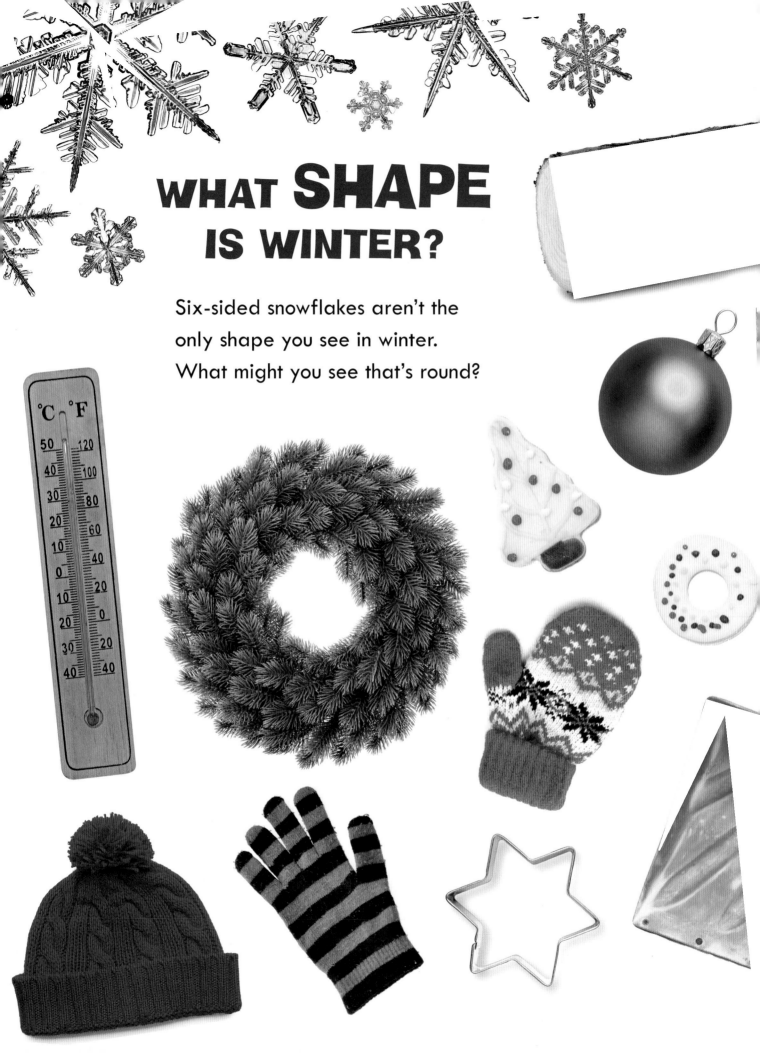

What do you see that's shaped
like a triangle or a rectangle?
What other shapes do you see?

DID YOU EVER WONDER HOW ICICLES FORM?

Icicles hanging from a roof form when the air temperature is below freezing, but sunshine warms snow or ice. The warmed snow melts and starts to drip down the roof. As the water drops reach the edge of the roof, they lose some of their heat to the cold air and freeze again. More drops from the roof melt and begin to follow the same path. They drip down the sides of the icicle and then refreeze, creating the long, thin icicle shapes.

WE WAIT FOR SNOW TO TRY SOME WINTER SPORTS.

People have lots of ways to move fast or slow on snow.

snowshoes

snowmobile

skis

sled

snowboard

SKATES LET PEOPLE SLIDE AND SPIN ON ICE.

Ice skates are shoes with thin metal blades attached to their soles. When the skater steps onto the ice, the movement of the blade and pressure from the skater's weight melts the ice just a little bit, creating a thin layer of water. Skaters glide and zoom smoothly and quickly because they're actually traveling on water, not hard, frozen ice.

PEOPLE DON'T ALWAYS WANT TO WAIT IN WINTER.

After snow falls, we can't always wait for it to melt before it's safe to walk on paths or drive on roads. So we use machines to move the snow.

A shovel combines two simple machines with no moving parts: a wedge and a lever. The shovel blade is the wedge, which digs into the snow. The shovel handle is the lever. The person shoveling provides the energy that makes this machine work.

A snowblower uses a motor to turn a blade that pulls snow into the machine and then throws it to the side. Snowblowers run on electricity or gasoline.

Snowplows use a large, angled blade to push snow to the side of the road. Plows are very heavy so that they can drive through snow. A snowplow can be 15 times heavier than an average car.

Of course, sometimes we move snow just for fun, like when we roll or throw snowballs. When you press snow, the ice crystals stick together to create new shapes.

WHAT DOES WINTER TASTE LIKE?

Bowls of hot soup, stew, or chili and cups of hot chocolate can warm us up in winter.

Mugs of mulled cider can, too. When you mull a drink, you warm it and add spices, such as cinnamon and cloves.

Many people also add orange or lemon slices.

Christmas

Hanukkah

Kwanzaa

WE CELEBRATE HEAPS
OF HOLIDAYS
ALL THROUGH
WINTER.

New Year's Eve and
New Year's Day

Martin Luther
King Jr. Day

Groundhog Day

Valentine's Day

St. Patrick's Day

Presidents' Day

AT LAST,
THE **WAITING**
AND **WONDERING**
COME TO AN END.

WONDERFUL WINTER
MAKES WAY FOR . . .

SPECTACULAR
SPRING.

SOME WONDERFUL
WINTER ACTIVITIES

six-pointed snowflakes

fake snow

snow globe

glitter icicles

pinecone bird feeder

ice spikes

FAKE SNOW

If you can't wait for real snow, make your own. Start with some disposable diapers that contain sodium polyacrylate. There's a pouch with white powder sewn into each diaper. Cut open the diapers to remove the powder and shake it into a bowl. Then add water to get instant snow. Sprinkle a few drops of water at a time until you get a texture you like. It will feel a bit cool, but pop it in the freezer for 10 minutes if you want even colder snow. (This "snow" is nontoxic, but don't eat it anyway.)

SIX-POINTED SNOWFLAKES

Start with a paper square. Fold the square in half vertically. Then fold the square in half horizontally twice. Open the two horizontal folds. Fold the lower left corner to touch the upper crease. Fold the upper left corner down to meet the paper edge. Then fold the shape in half horizontally. The point at the left will be the center of your snowflake. Cut off the paper opposite the point so that the edges are even. (Use safety scissors or ask an adult for help.) Cut shapes out of the folded edges. Open carefully to reveal your six-pointed snowflake.

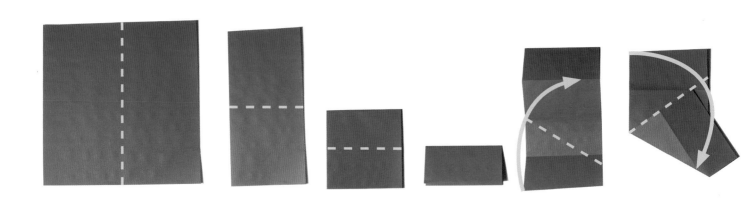

SNOW GLOBE

Fill about half a jar with clear corn syrup. Add some water (fill about half of the remaining space) and stir to dissolve the corn syrup. Add pinecones or other wintery objects. Sprinkle in some glitter or sequins, fill to the top with water, and stir again. Close the lid tightly. Shake to watch the snow swirl.

Optional: With adult supervision, use hot glue (or any waterproof glue) to attach a plastic figure to the bottom of the lid. You can also glue the lid onto the jar to keep your snow globe from opening.

GLITTER ICICLES

Tape a piece of construction paper inside a box lid. Tilt the lid so that it's at an angle. Squeeze glue in a line and watch it begin to drip down. Add more glue drips if you like. Then lay the lid flat and sprinkle the drips with lots of glitter. When the glue is dry, tip the lid and shake out the extra glitter. Remove the construction paper, and admire your sparkling icicles.

PINECONE BIRD FEEDER

Spread peanut butter on an open pinecone. Then roll the cone in birdseed, and hang your feeder from a tree branch.

 # ICE SPIKES

Freeze distilled water in an ice cube tray. You might get surprising ice spikes! They don't always happen, but they form more often than not. If you don't get any the first time, just thaw the ice and refreeze. Be sure to use distilled water; regular water doesn't usually make ice spikes.

To Dad and Roamer,
who take wonderful walks every winter's day
(and the rest of the year, too)

Thanks to Luca Ottaviano for his help modeling pseudosnow.

Henry Holt and Company, LLC
Publishers since 1866
175 Fifth Avenue, New York, New York 10010
mackids.com

Henry Holt® is a registered trademark of Henry Holt and Company, LLC.
Copyright © 2016 by Bruce Goldstone
All rights reserved.

Library of Congress Cataloging-in-Publication Data
Goldstone, Bruce, author.
Wonderful winter / Bruce Goldstone. — First edition.
pages   cm
Audience: Ages 4–8
ISBN 978-0-8050-9981-2 (hardcover)
1. Winter—Juvenile literature. 2. Winter—Pictorial works. I. Title.
QB637.8.G65 2016   508.2—dc23   2015030952

Our books may be purchased in bulk for promotional, educational, or business use.
Please contact your local bookseller or the Macmillan Corporate and Premium Sales Department
at (800) 221-7945 ext. 5442 or by e-mail at MacmillanSpecialMarkets@macmillan.com.

First Edition—2016 / Designed by April Ward and Anna Booth
Photo collages created with images from shutterstock.com, istockphoto.com, and Bruce Goldstone.
Printed in China by Toppan Leefung Printing Ltd., Dongguan City, Guangdong Province

1 3 5 7 9 10 8 6 4 2